HIDDEN IMAGES

HIDDEN IMAGES

DISCOVERING DETAILS IN THE WRIGHT BROTHERS' KITTY HAWK PHOTOGRAPHS 1900–1911

LARRY E. TISE

Charleston — London

the
History
PRESS

Published by The History Press
18 Percy Street
Charleston, SC 29403
866.223.5778
www.historypress.net

Cover image: A close-up look at an early glider flight.
Back cover inset: Orville Wright performing his "launching dance."

First published 2005

Manufactured in the United Kingdom

ISBN 1.59629.054.4

Library of Congress Cataloging-in-Publication Data

Tise, Larry E.
  Hidden images : discovering details in the Wright brothers' Kitty Hawk
photographs, 1900-1911 / Larry E. Tise.-- Limited ed.
      p. cm.
  Includes index.
  ISBN 1-59629-054-4 (alk. paper)
  1. Wright, Wilbur, 1867-1912--Photograph collections. 2. Wright, Orville,
1871-1948--Photograph collections. 3. Wright Flyer (Airplane)--Pictorial
works. 4. Aeronautics--United States--History--Sources. I. Title.
  TL540.W7T57 2005
  629.133'343'0222--dc22
                    2005017002

Notice: The information in this book is true and complete to the best of our knowledge. It is offered without guarantee on the part of the author or The History Press. The author and The History Press disclaim all liability in connection with the use of this book.

This catalogue was made possible with the generous support of the National Aeronautics and Space Administration (NASA) Office of Education and Langley Research Center, the staff and Friends of Joyner Library at East Carolina University and the Thomas Harriot College of Arts and Sciences of East Carolina University, Greenville, North Carolina. The original page layout and design was conceived by the staff of Joyner Library in 2004 and has been adapted by The History Press for this publication.

CONTENTS

PREFACE

This catalogue of hidden images from the photographs taken by Wilbur and Orville Wright at Kitty Hawk, North Carolina, between 1900 and 1911 would not have been compiled if my mother and father, Russell and Irene Norman Tise, had not been adventurous. Throughout my youth we took ghastly long—in distance, not time—but hugely informative and impressionable family vacations all over the eastern half of the United States.

I grew up in Winston-Salem, North Carolina. My parents took my sister and me to Nags Head and Kitty Hawk when I was not quite six years old, and we went to the Wright Brothers National Memorial. That was in 1948. How pleased I was that the first powered flight carrying a human being had taken place in the grand domain of the Tar Heel State.

Then, in the summer of 1949, they took us to Washington, D.C., where we visited the Arts and Industries Building of the Smithsonian Institution, or, as it was known until the 1950s, the National Museum. There I observed a somewhat tired and dusty bi-plane (that seemed to have been there forever) described as the first flyer of the Wright brothers from that important, epochal date of 17 December 1903, where they took flight on the sand flats before Big Kill Devil Hill at Kitty Hawk, North Carolina.

Some time in the early 1950s we went back to Kitty Hawk on a family vacation and I picked up a copy of Fred Kelly's official biography, *The Wright Brothers* (New York: Harcourt, Brace and Co., 1943), which has since been reprinted several times. I read it from cover to cover, lying on the sand under some shady umbrella, probably sipping a Dr. Pepper, and learned that the Smithsonian had only recently recognized the Wright brothers as the true pioneers of powered (or, as they then called it, "mechanical") flight. For those many years from 1903 until 1942, the Smithsonian Institution had declared that its former distinguished secretary, Samuel Pierpont Langley (1834-1906), had built, experimented with and proved the first man-carrying powered craft "capable of sustained flight." I was amazed to learn that I had been among the first Americans to see the 1903 Wright flyer in person and in place at the Smithsonian in 1949—with the age of flight well launched and, already, jet craft blasting the sound barrier above us, and with rockets to space and the moon on the horizon.

The Smithsonian's declaration about Langley's priority drove Wilbur and Orville Wright to total distraction. They bit their tongues and made brotherly eyebrow-raising and winking gestures of disrespect when they received the first Langley Medal of the Smithsonian on 10 February 1909, "for *advancing* [my emphasis] the science of aerodromes [Langley's word] in its application to aviation by their successful investigations and demonstrations of the practicability of mechanical flight by man."

This sleight of language so enraged them—why could they, they asked, not be declared the sole originators of heavier-than-air powered flight by man?—that they went to war with the Smithsonian—and, indeed, the world's aeronautical community—for almost forty years.

Although Wilbur died in 1912, Orville carried on the war. He was so offended that in 1928 he sent the original 1903 flyer to England to be exhibited at the National Science Museum of the United Kingdom at South Kensington near London, from 1928 until 1948. This was not because he thought the museum in London was a greater venue for the 1903 flyer. It was because he was so deeply enraged by the disingenuousness of his own national museum. He greatly preferred that the 1903 flyer should be displayed in perpetuity at the Smithsonian in Washington, D.C. He thus told the executors of his estate when he died in 1948 that the flyer should be brought back to America upon his death to be put on display at the Smithsonian with the following detailed inscription:

THE ORIGINAL WRIGHT BROTHERS AEROPLANE
THE WORLD'S FIRST POWER-DRIVEN,
HEAVIER-THAN-AIR MACHINE IN WHICH MAN
MADE FREE, CONTROLLED, AND SUSTAINED FLIGHT
INVENTED AND BUILT BY WILBUR AND ORVILLE WRIGHT
FLOWN BY THEM AT KITTY HAWK, NORTH CAROLINA
DECEMBER 17, 1903
BY ORIGINAL SCIENTIFIC RESEARCH THE WRIGHT BROTHERS
DISCOVERED THE PRINCIPLES OF HUMAN FLIGHT
AS INVENTORS, BUILDERS, AND FLYERS THEY
FURTHER DEVELOPED THE AEROPLANE,
TAUGHT MAN TO FLY, AND OPENED
THE ERA OF AVIATION

Should the inscription ever be altered, Orville, his executors and his advisors prescribed, the flyer would revert to his descendants and his estate.

It was good of Orville to make these arrangements so that I could see the Wright flyer in the summer of 1949 at the Smithsonian—and to make it look as if it had always been there.

My next encounter with the Wrights came in 1978, when I was director of what was then called the North Carolina Division of Archives and History, upon the seventy-fifth anniversary of the first flight. One of my legislative commanders in North Carolina at that time was Senator Melvin Daniels, cousin of John T. Daniels (1873-1948), the Kill Devil Hills lifesaver who took the now classic photograph of the first powered flight by human beings on 17 December 1903.

It was cousin Melvin who successfully introduced legislation in North Carolina around 1977 to place on North Carolina automobile license plates the slogan "First in Flight." This was a welcome relief from the previous slogan on North Carolina plates, "First in Freedom," which was roundly condemned by black descendants of slaves in my native state. Though I had not choosen the slogan "First in Freedom," I found myself in a position (as chief North Carolina historian) of having to explain its presence on state license plates. For good or ill, Senator Daniels's preferred slogan "First in Flight" has been on North Carolina license plates ever since. Congratulations, Senator Daniels, you served your historic relative well.

During the seventy-fifth anniversary of the first flight, I had the pleasure of working with William "Bill" Harris, then the superintendent of the Outer Banks Group of the National Park Service, including the Cape Hatteras National Seashore, Fort Raleigh on Roanoke Island and the Wright Brothers Memorial at Kitty Hawk. Bill and I had great fun planning the anniversary celebration, along with other Outer Banks notables including not only Senator Daniels, but also historian and worthy statesman David Stick and the late wily, capricious and beguiling Carolista Baum, who saved Jockey's Ridge forever as a state park on the Outer Banks. Carolista forced me to declare at the First Flight Society lunch on 17 December 1978 that we would somehow buy the full-scale replica of the1903 flyer—built by Ken Kellet of Colorado Springs, Colorado, which he tried (unsuccessfully) to fly at Kitty Hawk at the seventy-fifth anniversary—for exhibition in North

Carolina. Together Carolista and I, with various contributions, saved this good replica of flight; we also saved the Chicamacomico Lifesaving Station on Hatteras Island—the only place where visitors can see historic lifesaving techniques dramatically demonstrated today.

I enjoyed more Wright brothers' lore while I was director of the Benjamin Franklin National Memorial at the Franklin Institute in Philadelphia from 1989 until 1997. The Franklin Institute presented two awards to the Wright brothers, one in 1914 and another in 1933, for their pioneering efforts to produce flight. Orville, the shy member of the historic pair, made one of his last public addresses ever at the Franklin Institute on 20 May1914. The institute courted Orville for more than thirty years, beseeching him to donate the original 1903 flyer; but he desisted. But in that the Franklin Institute was one of the first engineering and scientific organizations to recognize the priority of the Wright brothers in flight, Orville willed to it the engineering drawings, the wind tunnel foils and much else that documented the Wright brothers' pioneering research on flight. While Orville was the more reserved member of the pair, he enjoyed his relationship with the scientific heads of the Franklin Institute and many other science organizations, and spent the thirty-six years after Wilbur died cavorting with such international stars of flight as Amelia Earhart (1897-1937) and Charles Lindbergh (1902-1974).

My next date with the Wright brothers' legacy came in 1998 or so, when I began consulting with friend and Congressman Martin Lancaster about potential federal legislation to provide for a national commemoration of the centennial of the first flight. Elizabeth Buford and Jeffrey Crow at the North Carolina Office of Archives & History welcomed my participation in plans for the centennial of the first flight in North Carolina. Admiral Ferg Norton and Dr. Kathryn Holton, successive directors of the First Flight Centennial Commission, were also welcoming and supportive partners in this research.

But the two individuals who made it possible for me to examine the Wright brothers *in extenso* were Dr. Samuel Massenberg, director of the Office of Education at the NASA Langley Research Center in Hampton, Virginia, and Professor Keats Sparrow, dean of the Thomas Harriot College of Arts and Sciences of East Carolina University. Both of these congenial practitioners of humanitarian genius and fellow researchers into little-known recesses of history and science have rewarded my curiosity about the Wrights—even though they did not know where my research was leading. Nor did I. That is perhaps one of the chief values of opportunities for scholarly research.

It was Keats Sparrow who introduced me to lebame houston and the Queen Barbara Hird. Barbara is a gifted actress who, among other credits, presided for many years in courtly fashion over the outdoor drama *The Lost Colony* at Manteo, North Carolina. It was helpful that lebame has blood from practically every strain of life on Roanoke Island and knows the faces of most of those folks—dead or alive. She introduced me to Mabel Evans Jones, who took an early important cue from the Wright brothers to enunciate the worthiness of Outer Banks residents. I will never forget the day that Keats Sparrow and I watched a recovered film copy of the 1920s silent version of *The Lost Colony*, pioneered, engineered and directed by Mabel Evans Jones. Also related to Mabel, lebame somewhat heroically re-ordered the letters in her name to declare her independence and her dedication to unique research on the history of Roanoke Island, Kitty Hawk and the larger realm of Outer Banks history.

What you will find in the following pages is an amalgam of my childhood and youthful enthusiasm, the endowment of my parents' peregrinations, my occasional research of the Wrights and extraordinary friendships with David Stick, Bill Harris, lebame houston and Barbara Hird; collegial kinships with KaLie Spiers and Sara Downing at the Outer Banks History Center in Manteo; many associations with the devoted professionals of the National Park Service; wise owl Leonard Bruno at the Library of Congress; lightning rod Tom Crouch at the National Air and Space Museum; and Deborah Galloway at the national First Flight Centennial Commission.

When I began working on the images found in this catalogue, I called upon the greatest font of knowledge on the subject and content of the Wright brothers' photographs at Kitty Hawk. That individual is none other than Bill Harris, currently the mayor of Kitty Hawk. Bill grew up in Kitty Hawk; his grandfather, Elijah Baum, was the first individual encountered by Wilbur Wright when he first arrived at Kitty Hawk in 1900. Not only did Bill grow up in the hallowed surroundings of the Wrights' exploits in flight, he also became an avid historian and student of the history of the area. While in school at Guilford College in the 1960s, he honed his skills as an oral historian by interviewing the old-timers of Kitty Hawk—both for their memories of the Wrights and for glimpses of the way they lived at the time the Wrights walked the sands around Kitty Hawk. When Bill chose a career, it was in the National Park Service where he eventually became superintendent of the Outer Banks Group.

Probably no one has studied the photographs taken by the Wright brothers at Kitty Hawk more than Bill Harris. It was thus a great pleasure to share the enhancements in this catalogue with him. In many cases my initial notions of what I thought I saw in some of the enhancements was corrected by Bill's wise instincts and his faultless knowledge of the lay of the land and arrangement of the waters surrounding the Outer Banks. It was in collaboration with him that I was able, ultimately, to attach names to the individuals who appear in many of these photographs. It was an enlightening event to visit with Bill and his computer and to see the vast store of information and knowledge he has accumulated about Kitty Hawk.

In fact, one of the most exciting and gratifying aspects of producing this unique catalogue was the experience of researching these photographs with Bill. With his constant and irrepressible humor it was, moreover, sometimes a hilarious escapade. If I have been the principal actor in launching this project and bringing it to conclusion, Bill has been the supporting actor whose knowledge and thorough explications of the Wrights' photographs at Kitty Hawk have made it possible.

While I live and work in Philadelphia, I must confess that I have had the happy incubational security of four institutions and the support of important directors at each of them during these past several years, making it possible for me to conduct this elongated and liberating research. At the National Aeronautics and Space Administration, Dr. Samuel Massenberg, director of education at NASA Langley Research Center; at East Carolina University, Dr. Keats Sparrow, dean of the Thomas Harriot College of Arts and Sciences; at Joyner Library at East Carolina University, where most of the enhanced images contained in this book were actually created, former library director Dr. Carroll Varner and the digital technical staff of the library; and with the Peter Gruber Foundation, St. Thomas, U.S. Virgin Islands, where Peter Gruber, chairman, and Patricia Murphy Gruber, president, inspired me to loftier and more ethereal realms of knowledge and achievement. These special individuals have made it possible for me to pursue some of my more iconoclastic interests in historical research.

Of course, I would never have found the hidden images published for the first time herein were it not for the many gainful and exciting hours with Glenn Woodell, creator of the Retinex software at NASA Langley Research Center, that introduced me to the possibilities of finding unnoticed images in the Wright brothers' photographs. But the real responsibility for the images that appear in this catalogue must go to Diana Williams, the past empress of East Carolina University's digitization program and an intrepid proofreader of the following text; and to the quiet and persistent Michael Reece, the most creative computer artist I have ever known. Michael and I worked together to find a world of photographic details that neither I nor anyone else knew existed. And it was this collaboration between historical research and technical expertise that allowed the hidden images in the following pages to be revealed.

Also crucial to this team of creative individuals was Vikram Ahmed, who helped us electronically navigate across many mediums to create a user friendly and easily searchable website for our Wright Brothers Digital Exhibit (http://www.lib.ecu.edu/exhibits/wright).

Grateful appreciation is hereby rendered to Douglas S. Smith, former communication officer for Joyner Library, and to Ginger D. Johnson, graduate marketing assistant, who designed the original layout for the pages that constitute this unique catalogue.

Thanks also to Larry, Nicholas, Nellie, Nona, David, Mort, Gretchen, Nancy, Vivian and all the other patient creatures on earth who have endured and kindly encouraged my rewarding intellectual meanderings with the Wrights.

Larry E. Tise
Wilbur and Orville Wright Visiting Distinguished Professor of History
Thomas Harriot College of Arts and Sciences
East Carolina University, Greenville, North Carolina

NOTE ON THE WRIGHT BROTHERS' PHOTOGRAPHS

Wilbur and Orville Wright have to be classed among the great amateur photographers of the early twentieth century. In addition to dabbling with the practice of shooting family outings and portraits, they began in the late 1890s to record scenes in nature, pastoral settings and people in action.

By 1900, when they made their first venture to North Carolina, they were already accomplished photographers. Making use of a large tripod camera that recorded images on either four-by-five-inch or five-by-seven-inch glass plate negatives, they lugged their camera and a case of blank glass plates to Kitty Hawk. There they exposed the glass plates on many scenes. But they knew not what they had recorded until they returned to Dayton.

In Dayton they had their own photo laboratory. They developed their own negatives and made their own prints, which they used to re-examine their activities at Kitty Hawk. But they also shared their prints with colleagues, friends and family. The surviving prints demonstrate their proficiency as photographers—they are crisp, clear and often surprisingly expressive of the object or scene photographed.

We are very fortunate that the Wrights made more than a few prints from their glass plate negatives, for in 1913 some of the glass plates were destroyed by a Dayton flood that inundated many of their precious historical treasures. The waters of the flood damaged many of the glass plates so severely that they were either defaced or obliterated. In 1949, according to the provisions of Orville Wright's will, the damaged glass plate negatives went to the Library of Congress. The prints from the estate eventually were given to Wright State University.

And, thus, a dilemma for the researcher of a book like *Hidden Images*. Glass plate negatives—if they are whole or even almost whole—are far superior to prints for scanning and the production of enhanced images. The glass plates often have details around the edges that were cropped out when prints were made. But in the absence of a whole glass plate or where details are obliterated from the glass plates, one must go to the prints to decipher what is missing.

Hence, in studying the Wright brothers' photographs one can easily become mildly schizoid. You can look at the Library of Congress glass plate images—which are now happily online—and you can study the Wright State print images—also online. But a print online is not like a glass plate online: people tend to scribble on prints. Some scribblers knew what they were talking about. Others were probably just guessing.

I found myself constantly wanting to check and verify potential interpretations of glass plates with the prints at Wright State. This investigative challenge could only be satisfied by holding the print or detailed scanned images of the glass plates. This catalogue is, therefore, an amalgam of what could be deciphered from both collections during a finite period of time.

In the end, I, with the assistance of my colleagues at NASA and East Carolina, studied every detail of every photograph made by the Wright brothers at Kitty Hawk. And wherever we found details in the photographs that enabled us to shed new light or additional perspective on Wrights' expereience at Kitty Hawk, we created dozens of enhanced images—many of them included in this book.

HIDDEN IMAGES

One can easily follow the track of my research between the glass plates and the prints: Library of Congress images have a three digit identifying number, e.g., #577; Wright State prints have a different kind of number, e.g., #15.7.33. All expanded numbers with suffixes such as 001 following Library of Congress photo numbers and such as D-1 and similar following Wright State identification numbers indicate hidden images.

I am most grateful to the benevolent czars of these collections for all of their assistance: Dr. Leonard Bruno, curator of aviation at the Library of Congress, whose career of research has tied together the period of the great editor of the Wright Papers, Marvin MacFarland, and our own era; and Dawne Dewey, director of special collections at Dunbar Library, Wright State University, who is a very knowledgeable expert on the location of Wright research materials worldwide. Without the wise and generous sharing of knowledge from these individuals and others already mentioned, this work would not have been possible.

INTRODUCTION

In late August 1900, Wilbur and Orville Wright made an uncharacteristically sudden decision to go to Kitty Hawk, North Carolina, to pursue the art and science of flight. They received their first information about the Kitty Hawk environs around 18 or 20 August from weather bureau Chief Joseph Dosher and former postmaster and Kitty Hawk promoter William J. Tate. On 6 September, Wilbur Wright departed Dayton, Ohio, as a strong and determined scout to open the way to Kitty Hawk, with Orville planning to follow later.

Never before had they crossed beyond the happy confines of the midwestern states of Ohio, Indiana, Iowa and Illinois. But they were driven by a passion to fly. Supported by a mother and a father who urged them to excel in whatever they chose in life—be it ministering, declaiming in politics, writing and printing or tinkering into the realm of engineering—the brothers never thought in small terms.

Ironically, neither Wilbur nor Orville graduated from high school. How odd in a family where their father and mother were both college educated; their older brothers Reuchlin (1861-1920) and Lorin (1863-1939) had been college students; and their younger sister Katharine (1874-1929) was a stellar graduate of Oberlin College, filled with the knowledge of Greek and Latin languages and classics.

Wilbur and Orville Wright were, throughout life, not very social beings. They talked to themselves and to a very few trusted friends. The only times they let down their guards was in delicious letters to their sister, Katharine, and in a few letters to fellow aviation pioneer George A. Spratt (1869-1934) of Coatesville, Pennsylvania. Otherwise, in all letters, conversations and electronic communications they were private and protective about their experiments at Kitty Hawk—even in their extensive correspondence with aviation pioneer Octave Chanute (1832-1910), one of their greatest fans and supporters.

Wilbur, the older brother, sometimes considered commanding and controlling, regularly criticized Orville. He thought Orville was sometimes careless, risking error and safety. Contrary to Wilbur's views, except for one dramatic crash at Fort Myer, Virginia, in 1908, Orville turned out to be one of the most cautious creatures in the history of flight. While Wilbur made guarded public appearances where he presented carefully written speeches, Orville evidently turned down almost every request to speak after an unhappy presentation in 1914 at The Franklin Institute.

Wilbur and Orville were unbelievably demanding of each other. They always felt that the other was slacking away from their prime mission, as evidenced in their sometimes harsh exchanges of letters while separated from each other in Europe and America on many occasions between 1907 and 1911. They could be merciless in their criticism of each other for mistakes made or for overlooked tasks. When Wilbur finally took their flying enterprise into the business realm with the establishment of the Wright Company in 1909 and with himself as president, Orville backed away from any position of leadership and mainly took care of routine business and production in Dayton as one of two vice presidents. When Wilbur died as a very young man in 1912, Orville grew more and more quiet until he sold the Wrights' business interests in 1915.

HIDDEN IMAGES

After Wilbur's death in 1912, Orville grew closer than ever to their sister Katharine. They lived in the same house, routinely traveled together and were closely dependent upon each other. After selling the flight business, Orville took Katharine and their aging father, Bishop Milton Wright (1828-1917), on a three-month summer vacation in 1916 to Georgian Bay in Canada. Orville loved the place so much he bought twenty-acre Lambert Island that summer, complete with a main house and six dependencies. He and Katharine returned every summer thereafter. Then suddenly in 1926, with the barest announcement, Katharine married Kansas City newspaper editor Henry Haskall—over Orville's objections. The marriage was of brief duration, as Katharine died of pneumonia on 3 March 1929.

Orville seems to have led a rather unhappy final two decades, quite lonely in the family home in Dayton and on annual summer trips to Canada. He maintained close personal friendships with old friends and business associates in Dayton and enjoyed close friendships with other stars of flight, including Amelia Earhart, Charles Lindbergh and General Henry "Hap" Arnold, one of his own pupils. And Orville was constantly in demand to appear as a special guest at events in Washington, Philadelphia, New York, Boston and often other places, including Dayton and Kitty Hawk. Although his letters with many individuals were warm, charming and playful, he often considered his load of correspondence burdensome. Particularly of interest to Orville in later years was a steady stream of letters from his old friends at Kitty Hawk—relationships that continued until his death from a heart attack in Dayton on 30 January 1948.

DISCOVERING KITTY HAWK
1900

While the brothers Wilbur (1867–1912) and Orville (1871–1948) Wright became fascinated with what they called "the problem of flight" perhaps as early as 1896, when they read about the daring flights of German pioneer Otto Lilienthal (1848-1896), they did not pursue their own efforts to fly until 1899, when they began searching for a place to conduct tests. Sons of a stern United Brethren (Methodist) minister, loners in a world of burgeoning technology, interested in their sister Katharine alone as the only female ever in their orbit, curious researchers and self-denying entrepreneurs on the make, the brothers Wright were ready to make a move on the world in 1900.

Based on their preliminary calculations, they needed a place remote from the prying eyes of reporters, with prevailing winds of twenty-plus miles per hour and soft sands for easy landings. Their prayers were answered in letters dated 16 and 18 August 1900, respectively from Joseph Dosher, stationmaster of the Kitty Hawk Weather Bureau, and William J. Tate, former postmaster and self-appointed local promoter of Kitty Hawk, North Carolina. Dosher informed them that they could find the climatic conditions they were seeking at Kitty Hawk quite readily, but there were no inns available for a lengthy stay. Tate wrote that Kitty Hawk would welcome them with open arms and that they could even stay at his house,which they did until they could establish a camp nearby.

When Wilbur departed Dayton on 6 September he followed what would become the brothers' hallowed pathway: taking a train from Dayton to Cincinnati and from there to Old Point Comfort at Hampton, Virginia; thence they proceeded to Norfolk, often to stay at the magnificent Monticello Hotel and thence to Elizabeth City, again via train. From Elizabeth City, where they got most of their foodstuffs and other necessities, to Kitty Hawk, the traveling got more difficult. In a letter home, Wilbur described his 1900 trip on Israel Perry's tiny boat *Curlicue* as a harrowing passage echoing the first Columbus venture to America—or perhaps even harking back to some of the Greek classics he knew almost by heart. Though his purpose was to entertain the Wrights still in Dayton, his letter revealed that he was really a landlubber, totally unskilled in matters of either navigation or flight at that time.

From 13 September until 2 October, Wilbur and Orville (who had arrived on 28 September) stayed at the home of William and Addie Tate. On 4 October they established a camp a half mile from Kitty Hawk and began taking pictures. Before departing Kitty Hawk on 23 October, they proceeded to Kill Devil Hills to practice in the even more favorable conditions of those windy hills.

A VIEW OF KITTY HAWK BAY

Kitty Hawk Bay in the distance—the first effort of the Wright brothers to capture in a photograph the locale of their 1900 experiments. The 1900 bay is green and luscious, serene and haunting—worthy of its beautiful name of Kitty Hawk, given to it originally in 1738. *Library of Congress #565.*

A closer look at the luscious Kitty Hawk Bay. *Hidden Image #565-001.*

DISCOVERING KITTY HAWK, 1900

WILLIAM J. TATE AND HIS FAMILY

Detail of the ornate folk art Kitty Hawk Post Office sign. *Hidden Image #546-001.*

Left: William J. ("Bill") Tate (1869–1953), former postmaster and congenial host of the Wrights in Kitty Hawk with daughter Irene on his lap. In the right portion of the photograph are Nancy Baum, a neighbor, Addie Sibbern Tate, wife and mother of Pauline, standing to her left. The family dog Spot surveys the scene. The Tates became lifelong supporters and friends of the Wrights. (Since the Library of Congress glass plate negative is badly damaged, both the glass plate negative and the Wright State photo are reproduced here.) *Library of Congress # 546.*

Right: Wright State photograph. *Wright State Library #15.5.25.*

HIDDEN IMAGES

Top left: Detail of Bill Tate and daughter Irene. Note newel post on staircase seen through doorway with a child's bonnet on the stairs, perhaps just torn off by the unhappy Irene who probably had never before posed for a picture. *Hidden Image #546-002.*

Top right: This very fine step to and from the front stoop is a shipping crate, handily adapted to a new purpose and held in place by a couple of two-by-four-inch stakes driven into the ground and nailed to the box. *Hidden Image #546-004.*

Bottom left: Detail of the very beautiful Addie Tate with Pauline and the rather stern looking Nancy Baum. Note the fine quality of the design and embroidery of the women's clothes. *Hidden Image #15.5.25 D2.*

Bottom right: This is the family dog Spot, curious as to the strange proceedings. *Hidden Image #15.5.25 D1.*

CAPTAIN AND MRS. JAMES HOBBS

Captain James Hobbs (1828–1918) who was "captain" by virtue of being keeper of the lifesaving station at Kitty Hawk, and his wife Eliza Hobbs (1833–1909), were especially close friends of the Wrights. Hobbs had been involved in a locally famous shootout in the 1880s. Wilbur and Orville made a special trip to the Hobbses' house on 17 December 1903 to inform them of their success earlier that day. *Library of Congress #547.*

Left: The Hobbses obviously had just had a new wood-shingle roof put on their house. The right-angle wooden slats held boards in place for piling shingles on before installation and to provide a resting place for roofers during their difficult work. *Hidden Image #547-002.*

Right: A close-up of this aging couple dearly beloved by the Wrights. *Hidden Image #547-001.*

CAMP KITTY HAWK IN ITS LUNAR LANDSCAPE

The 1900 Kitty Hawk camp was sparse indeed. This is a detail of the 1900 tent and the almost lunar landscape on which it was positioned. *Library of Congress #549.*

Close-up of the 1900 tent, proudly just put up and still empty, but in a photogenic setting next to a wind-swept tree. Note that there are no extra stability ropes tied to the trees or at the front of the tent, nor any of the wood reinforcements that would come later after the Wrights experienced a couple of storms. *Hidden Image #549-001.*

TENTING AT CAMP KITTY HAWK

Top left: The 1900 Kitty Hawk camp. Here, though the glass plate negative is badly damaged, one can view the neat cot arrangement of the first Wright camping trip to Kitty Hawk. *Library of Congress #560*.

Top right: Detail of the tent opening; inside can be seen a cot piled high with folded blankets. *Hidden Image #560-001*.

Left: Detail of tent reinforcements—diagonals on top, beams along the base on the side and back and a rope to the tree. *Hidden Image #560-002*.

THE WRIGHTS' ENVIRONMENT

The 1900 Kitty Hawk camp was a lunar landscape indeed. In this photograph, the Wrights were still exploring their new environment. *Library of Congress #564.*

A close-up of the camp, emphasizing the environment. Note the bare tree to the right. *Hidden Image #564-001.*

THE LUNAR LANDSCAPE

The "lunar" landscape viewed from the opposite side of the hill of the camp. Note the signature stark trees in the center. *Library of Congress #563*.

Detail of dead trees. *Hidden Image #563-001*.

A DISTANT VIEW OF KITTY HAWK VILLAGE

Left: An elegant view of Kitty Hawk in the distance from the Wright brothers' 1900 camp. Thoroughly exploring their new surroundings, the Wrights portrayed in photography the environment of their laboratory of flight. *Library of Congress #567*.

Above: Close-up of Kitty Hawk panorama. *Hidden Image #567-003*.

A somewhat closer view of structures in the village from the Wrights' camp. *Hidden Image #567-001.*

A fuzzy view of the eastern end of Kitty Hawk Bay. *Hidden Image #567-002.*

A CLOSER VIEW OF KITTY HAWK VILLAGE

Here is the only photographic full view of Kitty Hawk from 1900. The Wrights, excellent photographers, executed this beautiful still view of Kitty Hawk from their tenting camp. What may be seen in the details is the store in water to the left. A sailing watercraft next to the store; the residence of Jesse A. Cahoon (b.1838), first authorized Dosher grocer of the brothers Wright. Further yet, right in the mists of space, is the house and barn of Avery Benjamin Love Tillett (1861–1928), a lifesaver from Kill Devil Hills during the Wrights' 1901 venture. And then further to the right on stilts is a fish house, perhaps also belonging to Cahoon. *Library of Congress #568.*

The stilted fish house of Cahoon. *Hidden Image #568-002.*

In this detail, the Dosher Store in the water, with a sailboat adjacent, and the residence of Jesse Cahoon come into sharper focus. *Hidden Image #568-001.*

The house and barn of A.B.L. Tillett emerge from the mists. *Hidden Image #568-003.*

HIDDEN IMAGES

VIEW OF KITTY HAWK LIFESAVING STATION AND WEATHER STATION FROM THE 1900 CAMP

Left: When the Wrights turned from leeward to seaward, they got a spectacular view of the Kitty Hawk Lifesaving Station and the Kitty Hawk Weather Bureau. It was from these institutions that they reported their activities, flights and achievements. Though they moved in 1900 to their permanent base at Big Kill Devil Hill, Kitty Hawk remained their essential access to the outer world. *Library of Congress #557*.

Middle: A closer look at the lifesaving station on right and the weather station on the left. *Hidden Image #557-001*.

Bottom left: Another unidentified structure north of the Kitty Hawk stations. Note the fuzzy image of a telegraph pole to the right. *Hidden Image #557-002*.

Bottom right: Another fuzzy image of a structure to the north. *Hidden Image #557-003*.

Above: An even closer view of the Kitty Hawk Lifesaving Station. Note the distinctive lattice woodwork on the south end, and what appears to be a crane between the second and third structures. To the right of the station is the residence of station dog, Brownie. *Hidden Image #557-004.*

Below: An even closer view of the weather station. In this detail one can see the instrument-laden tower that rises above the structure. From this station the Wrights sent their famous message about their successful first powered flight on 17 December 1903. *Hidden Image #557-005.*

LIFESAVERS AT THE KITTY HAWK LIFESAVING STATION, 1900

The lifesavers of the Kitty Hawk Lifesaving Station in 1900. These mustachioed characters of all ages filled their civil service duties and gave vital assistance and entertainment to the brothers Wright upon their arrival at Kitty Hawk in 1900. *Left to right*: Robert Lee Griggs, Robert Fulton Sanderlin, Thomas Edward Hines, Joseph Edward Baum (the cook), Captain Samuel J. Payne, James Riley Best and Thomas Nelson Sanderlin. *Library of Congress #550*.

Left: Meet Robert Lee Griggs. *Hidden Image #550-003.*

Center: Robert Fulton Sanderlin. *Hidden Image #550-004.*

Right: Thomas Edward Hines. *Hidden Image #550-001.*

Left: Joseph Edward Baum was the cook at the station and not an official lifesaver. *Hidden Image #550-005.*

Center: Shifty-eyed Samuel J. Payne. *Hidden Image #550-002.*

Right: James Riley Best. *Hidden Image #550-006.*

SECOND VIEW OF LIFESAVERS AT KITTY HAWK, 1900

Left: A second, slightly different, view of the Kitty Hawk lifesavers, Note the addition of one new lifesaver in this photo: "Brownie," companion to the lifesavers. *Library of Congress #551.*

Right: The Kitty Hawk Lifesaving Station companion, Brownie. *Hidden Image #551-002.*

The lifesavers up close. *Hidden Image #551-003.*

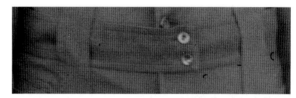

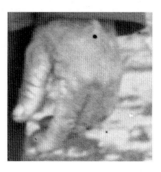

Upper left: A U.S. Lifesaving Service official patch from the uniform of Robert Lee Griggs. *Hidden Image #551-004.*

Bottom left and right: Detail of Thomas Sanderlin's hands, illustrating some of the rugged details of a lifesaver's appearance. *Hidden Image #551-007.*

Center: Thomas Sanderlin up close. *Hidden Image #551-001.*

Upper right: A U.S. Lifesaving Service hat. *Hidden Image #551-005.*

Middle right: Details of belt and buttons from the lifesavers' uniform. *Hidden Image #551-006.*

HIDDEN IMAGES

KITTY HAWK LIFESAVERS AT PRACTICE—GOING OUT

Left: The Wrights chose to record all they saw while at Kitty Hawk. Here the Kitty Hawk lifesavers are going out on a practice run on their lifesaving boat in rather calm surf. *Library of Congress #558*.

Below: The trip out up close. *Hidden Image #558-001*.

KITTY HAWK LIFESAVERS AT PRACTICE—COMING IN

Left: The Kitty Hawk lifesavers returning to shore; note that the surf has become slightly more turbulent. *Library of Congress #559*.

Below: A close-up of the return trip. *Hidden Image #559-001*.

Hidden Images

Thomas Tate, the First Wright Aviator

Thomas Tate (1888–1956) with a huge drum fish he had just caught. A seventy-pound youngster, Tate was the first human to fly on a Wright plane. In October 1900, he went aloft on the 1900 flyer. In the background of this photograph the 1900 glider and the tent lines can just be seen behind Tate. *Library of Congress #545.*

Close-up of the young Tate. *Hidden Image #545-002.*

Tom Tate's colorful, ornate suspenders. Note that every male photographed by the Wrights wore suspenders with intricate woven detail. *Hidden Image #545-001.*

HIDDEN IMAGES

AN ODD WRIGHT CAMERA GOOF

Though they were great amateur photographers, the Wrights could also make mistakes, as in the aim of the camera while taking this photograph. Their 1900 glider is barely visible at the extreme right of this picture. Indeed, in most prints from this glass plate negative the glider has been inadvertently cropped out. *Library of Congress #561.*

Close-up of the almost missed glider. *Hidden Image #561-001.*

THE WRECK AND THE STATION COMPLEX BEYOND

Although we are intended to focus on the failed 1900 flying craft, which crashed on 10 October 1900 in high winds gusting to thirty miles per hour, there are other images in this photo. Off in the left corner are some of the buildings adjacent to the Kitty Hawk Lifesaving Station with either the flag pole or a telegraph pole visible. On that day the Wrights had tried to fly their glider as a kite attached to a wooden derrick. They attached many lines to the derrick so that they could practice guidance and control on the glider. When the glider broke away in the strong wind many lines were pulled away and may be seen next to the wreck in this photograph. *Library of Congress #544.*

Left: Image of beachfront buildings south of Kitty Hawk Lifesaving Station. *Hidden Image #544-001.*

Right: A close-up of broken lines on the right side of the crashed plane. *Hidden Image #544-001.*

DISCOVERING KILL DEVIL HILLS

After the wreck of 10 October, the Wrights never again used a derrick and they forever after called the site of the crash "Hill of the Wreck." They immediately repaired their machine and on 19 October proceeded to Big Kill Devil Hill, four miles south of Kitty Hawk, where they achieved this spectacular flight of the 1900 glider. Again, while the focus of the photograph is on the glider, in the lower left corner is the almost obscured Kill Devil Hills Lifesaving Station, revealing for the first time the extent of the complex surrounding the station. *Library of Congress #556.*

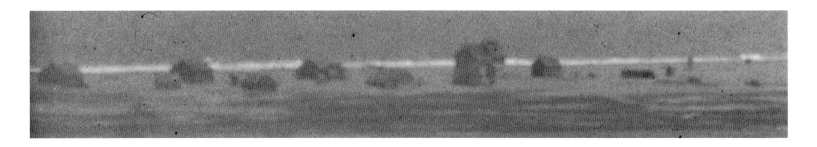

The first Wright image of the Kill Devil Hills Lifesaving Station complex. The largest of the buildings is the lifesaving station. *Hidden Image #556-001.*

THE MAJESTY OF KILL DEVIL HILLS

In awe of the great winds they discovered at Big Kill Devil Hill, the Wrights' last photograph of 1900 was this panorama of the Kill Devil Hills. Again the almost obscure image of the Kill Devil Hills Lifesaving Station is observable in the left corner. *Library of Congress #566.*

Detail of image of Kill Devil Hills Lifesaving Station. *Hidden Image #566-001.*

BASE CAMP KILL DEVIL HILLS
1901

Between 23 October 1900, when the Wrights departed Kitty Hawk, and 7 July 1901, when they left Dayton for another season of flight, there were several major developments.

First, Wilbur and Orville conceived an improved flyer and discussed their plans by letter with flight pioneer Octave Chanute, and in person when the great Chanute traveled to Dayton in June to meet the brothers. The most knowledgeable person on the history of flight and on individuals around the world attempting to fly, Chanute (1835–1910) was glad to get to know the Wrights and was impressed from the onset with their ingenuity and hard work.

At this time, Wilbur and Orville also decided to move their testing operations from the Kitty Hawk vicinity to Big Kill Devil Hill. But so as to avoid the annoyance of living in a tent as they had during their stay in 1900, they decided to build their first wooden building at the base of the hill. This required land (which was offered them without cost by the owner); building materials, hardware and tools (which Bill Tate helped to secure from Elizabeth City); a well for fresh water; and an endless number of other incidental items. The brothers left for Kitty Hawk on 7 July to begin work on constructing their camp.

At the suggestion of Chanute, two other young would-be aviators were invited to spend time with the Wrights at Kitty Hawk. Edward C. Huffaker (1856–1936) of Chuckey City, Tennessee, had worked at the Smithsonian Institution on the design of small-scale flying models. But he also had built a glider for Chanute that was to be tested in the summer of 1901. Huffaker was with the Wrights from 18 July until 18 August. The other aspirant to visit the brothers at Kitty Hawk was George A. Spratt (1869–1934) of Coatesville, Pennsylvania, trained in medicine, but really a technological tinkerer and dreamer. Spratt arrived on 25 July and stayed until on 16 August.

Huffaker maintained a detailed diary of everything that happened at the camp in 1901, thus inspiring the Wrights to keep their own diaries beginning in 1902. Spratt's inquiring genius into the theories of flight fired discussions in the camp and a subsequent spate of letters with the Wrights in the months and years that followed. Even Chanute made an appearance from 4 to 11 August and kept detailed engineering statistics on all flights while he was at the camp. The tables of data he prepared on their flights subsequently aided the Wrights in making their own calculations.

The other regular at the camp in 1901 (and also 1902 and 1903) was Dan Tate (1865–1905). Half-brother of Bill Tate and father of Tom Tate, Dan was the Wrights' regular paid general assistant at the camp—that is, on the days he showed up. Tate's penchant for arriving late, for laying out of work and his occasional sudden disappearances to go fishing left the Wrights unable to proceed with their experiments.

With this considerable assembly of knowledge, assistance and enthusiasm in the camp, the Wrights conducted perhaps as many as one hundred flights in 1901, covering distances of up to four hundred feet. It was a frustrating period for them, for the 1901 glider did not perform up to their expectations. But with the presence of Spratt and Chanute particularly, Orville and Wilbur developed a cadre for both discussion and experimentation that would continue until they had solved the problem of flight.

HIDDEN IMAGES

THE 1901 WRIGHT CAMP FROM ATOP BIG KILL DEVIL HILL

The 1901 camp seen from the top of Big Kill Devil Hill. This photograph was taken after a heavy rainstorm. By this time the Wrights had completed construction on their first wooden building, which they used both as a workshop and their dormitory. The adjacent tent, which they had used in 1900, was set up for the three guests who would be with them much of the flying season. Designation of the camp on this print is in the handwriting of Orville Wright. *Wright State #15.7.20*.

Detail of the camp and its immediate surroundings. *Hidden Image #15.7.20 D1*.

BASE CAMP KILL DEVIL HILLS, 1901

A CLOSER VIEW

Left: This closer view of the 1901 camp appears to have been made about the same time as the photograph of the camp (*opposite*), but is not one of the better Wright photographs. *Library of Congress #576.*

Below: This close-up adds little detail, but reveals the openness of the Wrights' shop building. *Hidden Image #576-001.*

HIDDEN IMAGES

HAMAN HOUSE—ONE OF THE RETREATS FOR THE WRIGHTS

Left: This is a view from the 1901 Wright camp looking to the west, in the direction of Roanoke Sound. A unique feature of this photograph is that it shows a building that may be, as evidenced by its surroundings, the Haman House, or Hamans, on Hamans Bay (locally spelled Hayman), frequently mentioned by the Wrights. The house was abandoned by the time the Wrights arrived in 1900, but they frequently took walks there because it was such a great place to observe the abundant bird population that inhabited that area of the Roanoke Sound. They also used it as a retreat during an occasional fast-moving storm. The building visible in this image may not be Hamans, but instead a fish house on the marshy grounds between Kill Devil Hills and Colington Island. In any case, it is very close to Hamans. *Library of Congress #578.*

Right: A closer look at what might be the Haman House. *Hidden Image #578-001.*

THE SAND CRAB

Left: The Wrights occasionally diverted their camera to natural life on the Outer Banks, such as in this extraordinary 1901 photograph of a sand crab. The details of the crab's eyes and legs show the faithful clarity of many of their photographs. *Library of Congress #579.*

Right: The crab's hairy, muscular legs. *Hidden Image #579-002.*

Above: A surreal view of the crab's eyes. *Hidden Image #579-001.*

HIDDEN IMAGES

KITTY HAWK AS A SALON ON FLIGHT

Left: By early August in 1901, the Wright camp became pretty crowded and during bad weather turned into a virtual salon on flight. Visible within this photograph, seated on the cot on the left are Octave Chanute, Orville Wright and Edward Huffaker. Wilbur Wright seems to be leading the discussion, and various workbenches, tools and rain gear can be seen in the background. To the left of the building in front of the tent is a special pump, sunk in the sand, to provide fresh water. Orville claimed the pump produced the best water in Kitty Hawk. George Spratt, who is missing from the picture, evidently handled the camera. *Library of Congress #581*.

Bottom left: Wilber leads the discussion. *Hidden Image #581-002*.

Bottom right: A closer look at four of the five hopeful aviators. *Hidden Image #581-001*.

THE CHARACTERS OF KITTY HAWK, 1901

Left: In this photograph from the same perspective as the image opposite, Orville has slipped from the scene to take the picture. Huffaker is here seated to the left with Chanute next to him. Wilbur has not moved, but Spratt has taken a position seated next to the front door with his notebook in hand. *Library of Congress #583.*

Below: The camp water pump with a washbasin located on a handy custom-made shelf. *Hidden Image # 583-001.*

Bottom left: A close-up of Edward Huffaker. *Hidden Image #583-003.*

Bottom right: George Spratt deep in contemplation with notebook in hand. Behind him, outside of the building, a the collection of whelk and other shells that the Wrights gathered to take back to Dayton for their nephews and nieces. *Hidden Image #583-002.*

HIDDEN IMAGES

WILBUR WRIGHT DRAGS THE TARPAPER PROCESSION AS ORVILLE DRESSES FOR THE OCCASION

Left: This photograph may have been made with a camera brought by Chanute in 1901 to Kitty Hawk. His images lack the clarity of most of the Wrights' photographs, but are clearly companions to the preceding images of the camp. Here Wilbur, in white shirt and finery, appears to drag a piece of roofing tarpaper—a certain source of nasty black smudges on hands and clothes. In the background, behind him, the cots have been removed from the tent to be aired. Huffaker is seated on a cot under the awning with some records. In the shadows of the building can be seen a faint image of Orville tying his bowtie, perhaps readying himself to help Wilbur with the tarpaper! *Wright State #15.5.22.*

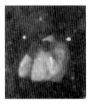

Right: Orville in the shadows, affixing his tie. *Hidden Image #15.5.22 D2.*

Bottom right: Close-up of Wilbur with the tarpaper; note the empty bunks behind him. *Hidden Image #15.5.22 D1.*

Bottom left: Edward Huffaker poses for the photo, holding a sheaf of paper files in his hands. *Hidden Image #15.5.22 D3.*

ORVILLE DISPLAYS THE 1901 GLIDER PILED ON END

Above: Orville poses with the 1901 glider turned on its end to demonstrate the large size of the machine. The slope of Big Kill Devil Hill can be seen in the background. *Library of Congress #574.*

Right: Close-up of Orville balancing the glider. *Hidden Image #574-001.*

Hidden Images

Wilbur and Orville Fly the 1901 Glider as a Kite
If It Would Not Fly as a Kite, It Would Not Fly as a Plane №1

Above: Wilbur on the left and Orville on the right fly the 1901 glider as a kite at the foot of Big Kill Devil Hill. *Library of Congress #571*.

Right: Close-up of Wilbur in action. *Hidden Image #571-001*.

WILBUR AND ORVILLE FLY THE 1901 GLIDER AS A KITE
IF IT WOULD NOT FLY AS A KITE, IT WOULD NOT FLY AS A PLANE №2

Above: Another view of the "kite" flying, this time with Wilbur in the background and Orville in the foreground. *Library of Congress #580.*

Right: Close-up of the brothers and the nose cone of their craft. *Hidden Image #580-001.*

THE ASCENSION OF BIG KILL DEVIL HILL

Left: While this photograph appears to be an image of the natural setting at Kill Devil Hill, in the detail of this picture two people can be seen ascending the hill for a flight of the 1901 glider. *Library of Congress #575*.

Right: Closer view of the intrepid climbers. *Hidden Image #575-001*.

LAUNCH READINESS

Left: Another photograph seeming to be of Big Kill Devil Hill reveals in detail that the two figures—surely Wilbur and Orville—are on top of the hill ready for a test flight. *Library of Congress #569.*

Right: Closer view of the brothers and their craft ready to take the plunge. *Hidden Image #569-001.*

Hidden Images

Experimental Landings

Here Wilbur has landed the 1901 glider after a test flight, whether from Big Kill Devil Hill is not clear. In the foreground there seem to be a matching pair of indentations of the frontal apparatus of the craft, suggesting that the glider may have been repositioned for the photograph. This image is somewhat emblematic of how the Wrights felt when they left Kitty Hawk on 20 August 1901. Due to their limited success, they were discouraged about achieving flight. *Library of Congress #570.*

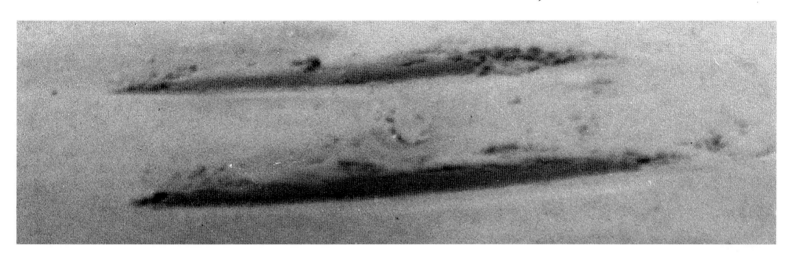

Above: Telltale marks of a previous landing. *Hidden Image #570-002.*

Below: Close-up of Wilbur on the landed 1901 flyer. Note Wilbur's long, wiry fingers. *Hidden Image #570-001.*

THE CONQUEST OF FLIGHT
1902

When Wilbur and Orville left Kitty Hawk in 1901, there was doubt in their minds as to whether they would further pursue the subject of flight. They were exceedingly quiet about the results of their tests when they got back to Dayton. However, once again Chanute stepped in to encourage the brothers. He sent his calculations on their 1901 test flights at Kitty Hawk, which enabled them to determine that their existing calculations of air pressures on curved surfaces appeared to be off the mark.

Chanute also invited Wilbur to give an address to the Western Society of Engineers in Chicago in September 1901. This challenge to describe just what the Wrights had learned seemed to spur them back into experimentation, this time on airfoils connected to bicycles in their Dayton shop. They moved on to the use of a wind tunnel before the end of the year. They also began testing engines that might be used on a powered flyer.

In the early months of 1902, the brothers began designing an entirely new flying machine based on these studies and the calculations they shared with Chanute. By early August they had completed the construction of components of the new glider and began packing the parts for a new venture to Kitty Hawk.

In 1902 Orville and Wilbur spent their longest period yet at Kitty Hawk, departing Dayton on 25 August and arriving on the twenty-eighth. They would remain until 28 October. As in 1901, they rebuilt their camp, put in a full-scale kitchen and made it much more habitable. This construction and rennovation took longer than a week. They then dismantled the 1901 glider and reused many of its parts in the new machine. By 19 September they were ready to begin testing.

Again, the Wrights were far from alone at Kitty Hawk. Their older brother Lorin came for a two-week visit at the end of September. On 1 October their friend George Spratt returned and stayed for three weeks. On 5 October Chanute and his new assistant Augustus M. Herring (1867–1926), a future unscrupulous rival for the title of inventing flight, arrived to test a new machine developed for Chanute. The pair would only remain in Kitty Hawk ten days, but that was long enough for Herring to later claim that the Wrights stole his ideas.

This was an incredibly eventful and inventive time for the Wrights and for the birth of flight. The Wrights made between seven hundred and a thousand glides between 19 September and 24 October. Their distances increased to 622 feet and flight times to 26 seconds. By the end of September Orville was quietly telling his sister Katharine that he and Wilbur had solved the problem of flight. He was sure that with a little more practice, without distractions, both of them would master the controls in their new machine.

REORGANIZING KITTY HAWK FOR FLIGHT

Left: This photograph was taken on 29 August 1902, the day the Wrights returned to their camp at Kitty Hawk. It reveals Wilbur beginning the reconstruction of the camp building, with the 1901 glider stored from the past year on the right—before it was dismantled to provide parts for the 1902 machine. This amazingly complex photograph reveals many details. *Wright State #15.7.21.*

Bottom right: In the center of the room sits two heavy wooden and metal-reinforced trunks—one with a medical satchel on top. *Hidden Image #15.7.21 D3.*

Bottom center: A handsaw stored atop the 1901 flyer. *Hidden Image #15.7.21 D5.*

Bottom left: This detail shows a rug or quilt hanging in the rafters—probably as protection against marauding mice and other varmints. *Hidden Image #15.7.21 D7.*

Left: Wilbur Wright, perhaps pondering how to make sense out of this place, with covers pulled off of stored items and with their gas stove situated on the floor in the center. *Hidden Image #15.7.21 D1.*

Bottom left: A pile of covers from the camp on the left with a binoculars case on top. *Hidden Image #15.7.21 D4.*

Bottom right: Perhaps the most important detail from the photograph: on the shelf in the center of the room what appears to be an open notebook with pen inserted—surely the beginnings of Orville Wright's diary and notebooks for the 1902 testing season. *Hidden Image #15.7.21 D2.*

THE REASSEMBLED KITCHEN

Left: This photograph, taken in early September 1902, shows the dramatic transformation brought to the disorganized space shown on the preceding pages. *Wright State #15.7.22.*

Bottom right: Good Chase and Sanborn coffee was on hand and properly stored. *Hidden Image #15.7.22 D1.*

Bottom left: Flour and potatoes were in abundance. *Hidden Image #15.7.22 D2.*

Above: A shelf of canned vegetables and of cups, saucers and all else. *Hidden Image #15.7.22 D4.*

Left: The gas stove has been reassembled with the oven on top of the burner units; the brand name "Reliable" is clearly revealed. *Hidden Image #15.7.22 D3.*

Center: The old "Reliable" up close. *Hidden Image #15.7.22 D5.*

Right: Two lanterns are easily accessible—one for inside light and the other for ventures out-of-doors. *Hidden Image #15.7.22 D6.*

THE REASSEMBLED SLEEPING SPACE

Left: While the Wrights renovated their kitchen space, they also moved their sleeping bunks to the rafters of the building, creating what they called jokingly their "patent" beds. Details show that they were well equipped with comfortable sheets, blankets and quilts hanging on the wall above the beds. This picture, taken on 6 September 1902, shows that the brothers were ready for a comfortable flying season. *Wright State #16.3.23.*

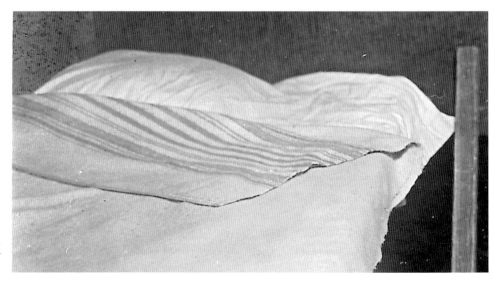

Right: Detail of new sleeping quarters at Kill Devil Hills in 1902. *Hidden Image #16.3.23 D1.*

THE 1902 WORKSHOP/DORMITORY/LIVING SPACE COMPLETE

Above: In this 1902 print, the considerable enlargement of the 1901 camp building can be seen in the change in roofing pattern between the two segments of the completed building. The Wrights' efforts to shore up the buildings from constant sinking in the sands can be seen in the fairly elaborate system of undergirding and side supports. The method of construction is also clear: a board-and-batten design, identical to the lifesaving stations near by. The pump has returned, and in this image one can see the workshop area, complete with tools, created next to the kitchen. Here Wilbur appears to be sewing together parts of the new 1902 craft. *Library of Congress #593.*

Right: Wilbur Wright, busy sewing. Note the kitchen to his right. *Hidden Image #593-001.*

THE LIFESAVERS OF KILL DEVIL HILLS, 1902

Left: During most of their trips to Kitty Hawk, the Wright brothers were quite dependent upon the knowledge, wisdom and frequent services of the lifesavers from the Kill Devil Hills Lifesaving Station as shown in this magnificent photograph of the main building of the station. The men pictured here, left to right, are: William Thomas Beacham (most likely), John T. Daniels, "Uncle" Bennie O'Neal and Adam T. Etheridge (1873-1940). Not shown here are Captain Jesse Ward, Robert Wescott (1869-1925)and Willie St. Clair Dough (1870-1931), who would also play important roles in the Wrights' achievements in 1902, 1903 and 1908. *Library of Congress #600.*

Opposite bottom left: The station signal bell was used to call the lifesavers from the various quarters where they lived in the complex. *Hidden Image #600003.*

Opposite bottom middle: The majestic lifesaving boat, dramatically poised to be wheeled across the sand to turbulent shores; note the telegraph pole just behind the boat. *Hidden Image #600002.*

Opposite bottom right: One cannot help but note the empty and broken windows on the second level, surrounded by simple, but dignified Victorian woodwork and an observation deck. *Hidden Image #600005.*

Above: A close-up of the Kill Devil Hills lifesavers. *Hidden Image #600-004.*

Left: There is a mysterious, unidentified artwork behind the lifesaver Adam Etheridge. *Hidden Image #600-001.*

THE SUCCESSFUL TEST SEQUENCE

On 19 September 1902 the new glider was ready for testing. The Wrights, with the assistance of Dan Tate, took the craft out to test it as a kite and immediately achieved this dramatic success. This photograph—one of the most elegant in the series—not only shows the graceful glider in flight, but also Dan Tate's colorful outfit of all-weather hat, checkered shirt, richly colored suspenders and handkerchief protruding from his back pocket. In the background one can see an almost smug sense of success in Wilbur's face as he barked out orders to Tate and waited for Orville to take this great picture. *Library of Congress #631*.

Left: Dan Tate and Wilbur Wright up close. *Hidden Image #631-001*.

Middle: Wilbur in his glory. *Hidden Image #631-003*.

Right: Dan Tate's suspenders. *Hidden Image #631-004*.

WILBUR WRIGHT ALOFT

Left: On 2 October 1902 the Wrights had a successful flight from Big Kill Devil Hill, as shown in this image of Wilbur Wright. *Library of Congress #630.*

Below: Close-up of the flyer. *Hidden Image #630-001.*

THE CONQUEST OF FLIGHT, 1902

WILBUR WRIGHT SOARING

Left: By 10 October the Wright brothers were almost seasoned flyers, as revealed in this magnificent view of Wilbur aloft from Big Kill Devil Hill. *Library of Congress #602.*

Below: Close-up of glider flight of 10 October 1902. *Hidden Image #602-001.*

ORVILLE WRIGHT SOARS AS WELL

On that same day, 10 October, Orville took his turn (Wilbur did nearly all of the flying until 1902). In this very telling photograph, Wilbur on the left and Dan Tate on the right assist Orville's take off. To the far left one can see rival Augustus M. Herring standing with hand on hip in seeming amazement; while then-friend George Spratt rests on the sand. This picture must have been taken by Lorin Wright who was still in Kitty Hawk at that time. Octave Chanute, the only other participant, is missing from this panoramic photograph. *Library of Congress #592.*

THE CONQUEST OF FLIGHT, 1902

Top left: George Spratt loafs on the sandy slope as the Wrights launch their 1902 craft. Augustus Herring stands with his arm to his hip, perhaps in disbelief of what is happening in his presence. *Hidden Image #592-001.*

Top right: Orville pilots the plane. *Hidden Image #592-003.*

Bottom left: Wilbur helps get the craft aloft. *Hidden Image #592002.*

Bottom right: Dan Tate assists the launch. *Hidden Image #592-004.*

THE ORIGINAL FIRST FLIGHT CELEBRATION

At the end of the most amazing day in the history of flight to that time, the 1902 Kitty Hawk contingent gathered to celebrate the triumphs of the day. *Wright State #15.7.2.*

Close-up of the 1902 participants. *Left to right*: Octave Chanute, with his camera box to his right; Orville; Wilbur, with his tie blowing in the wind; Herring, in cap; Spratt, with hat; and Dan Tate in his all-weather hat at the far end of the 1902 flyer. *Hidden Image 15.7.2 D1.*

Left: Octave Chanute. *Hidden Image 15.7.2 D2.*

Center: Orville Wright. *Hidden Image 15.7.2 D3.*

Right: Wilbur Wright *Hidden Image 15.7.2 D4.*

Left: Augustus M. Herring. *Hidden Image 15.7.2 D5.*

Center: George A. Spratt. *Hidden Image 15.7.2 D6.*

Right: Dan Tate. *Hidden Image 15.7.2 D7.*

WILBUR SOARS EVEN LONGER

Above: Wilbur is again sent aloft on 10 October as Dan Tate chases his progress across the top of Big Kill Devil Hill. *Library of Congress #597*.

Right: Dan Tate chases Wilbur's flight. *Hidden Image #597-001*.

THE CONQUEST OF FLIGHT, 1902

WILBUR OVER KILL DEVIL HILLS

Left: Once skyward, Wilbur soars with a very clear image of the Kill Devil Hills Lifesaving Station and complex seen in the distance under his wings. This is one of the finest images of the station. *Wright State #15.6.46.*

Below: The Kill Devil Hills Lifesaving Station revealed. *Hidden Image #15.6.46 D1.*

THE CHANUTE FLYER DEBACLE, 13 OCTOBER 1902

On 13 October 1902, the time came to test Chanute's new three-wing oscillating glider. After testing it successfully as a kite that morning, Augustus M. Herring served as pilot for this minimally successful flight, with the assistance of Dan Tate on the right and perhaps Orville on the left. After having watched the dramatic and successful Wright flights over previous days, both Herring and Chanute quickly gave up on the machine. *Wright State #15.6.2.*

Dan Tate follows the glider. *Hidden Image #15.6.2 D3.*

Close-up of the Chanute flyer—the only time it momentarily left the ground. *Hidden Image #15.6.2 D1.*

Orville Wright, perhaps helping with the launch of Chanute's glider. *Hidden Image #15.6.2 D2.*

WRIGHT TRIALS RESUME

Left: Wilbur and Orville's exciting glider flights quickly resumed, as Wilbur here ascends over the abandoned Chanute machine. *Hidden Image #15.6.9 D1.*

Below: Abandoned Chanute flyer in the distance. *Hidden Image #15.6.9 D2.*

Another Triumphal Flight

Above: On 18 October Orville and Dan Tate launch Wilbur on another triumphal flight. *Hidden Image #15.6.5 D1.*

Right: Close-up of Orville's launching dance. *Hidden Image #15.6.5 D2.*

CONTROLLED FLIGHT

Left: The triumph of the Wrights is further demonstrated on 24 October as Wilbur makes this impressive controlled turn using the creative devices he and Orville had originated. *Library of Congress #598*.

Below: Close-up of the world's first entirely controlled flight. *Hidden Image #598-001*.

POWERED FLIGHT
1903

The Wrights returned to Dayton on 31 October 1902 feeling triumphant. So confident were they that they had solved the problem of flight, Orville and Wilbur began preparing an application for a patent on "the flying machine." The Wrights believed the problem of flight rested in lift, drift and control and not necessarily in the application of power. And when they got their comprehensive patent it was based on these general principles.

Nevertheless, after their successful glider flights at Kitty Hawk in 1902 they began to work immediately on developing a powered flyer. In November and December 1902 they tested their engine and the design of propellers. This work continued during the first six months of 1903. On 24 June 1903 Wilbur gave another lecture to the Western Society of Engineers titled "Experiments and Observations in Soaring Flight," describing what he and Orville were learning at Kitty Hawk.

On 23 September 1903 the Wrights headed back to Kitty Hawk, where they planned to add a second building to their flight-testing complex. Although construction activities continued until 5 October, they had the 1902 glider ready for new tests by 28 September. The glider tests continued until 12 November, when use of the 1902 glider had to be terminated due to its condition. But not before two hundred additional glides had been performed, with modifications to the craft producing amazing results.

On 9 October 1903 the Wrights began assembling a new powered flyer. Their progress was hampered by broken propeller shafts, requiring Orville to return to Dayton to secure new shafts made from steel rather than aluminum; he would not return to Kitty Hawk until 11 December.

Meanwhile, the Wrights had invited only two individuals to join them at Kitty Hawk for the 1903 season, confidants George Spratt and Octave Chanute. Spratt arrived on 23 October and assisted in glides and assembly of the 1903 machine. When the propeller shafts broke, he left the next morning, somewhat disappointed, but also offering to help ship the broken shafts back to Dayton.

At Manteo, a frequent stopover for visitors to the Outer Banks, Spratt encountered Chanute, who was on his way to Kill Devil Hills. When Chanute arrived on 6 November he was also disappointed not to see powered flight tests, but during the seven days he was in camp he discussed grand future plans for his new tests and for getting the Wrights to do public displays of flight. He left Kitty Hawk on 12 November.

Upon Orville's return with the new steel shafts, the Wrights reassembled the glider and quickly resumed the tests. On 14 December the brothers placed their launching track on the slope of Big Kill Devil Hill. With the assistance of five men from the Kill Devil Lifesaving Station, Wilbur attempted a flight that lasted 3.5 seconds and traveled 105 feet. But the plane settled quickly to surface and this test was considered a failure.

After repairs were made, additional tests were conducted and on 17 December four famous successful flights were accomplished. The Wrights immediately sent a telegram from the Kitty Hawk Weather Station back to Dayton announcing their accomplishments. By 21 December they had packed up the 1903 flyer and were headed back to Dayton and to world fame.

THE 1903 UPGRADED LIVING QUARTERS

Left: When the Wrights returned to Kitty Hawk in 1903 they again expanded their building stock. They added a second building to serve as their hangar for the 1903 powered flyer. This also enabled them to upgrade their kitchen and living area with more carpeting, seating and even a place to rest their reading materials, here a copy of *Scientific American*. *Wright State #16.3.22.*

Below: The 31 October 1903 issue of *Scientific American* surely had just arrived in the camp at Kitty Hawk. *Hidden Image #16.3.22 D1.*

POWERED FLIGHT, 1903

MORE FLIGHTS OF THE 1902 GRACEFUL GLIDER

Left: The Wrights continued conducting flights with the 1902 glider. This October 1903 image shows Wilbur high over the new camp, now complete with their two substantial buildings—newly finished and ready for use. *Wright State #15.6.40.*

Below: Close-up of the 1903 camp. *Hidden Image #15.6.40 D1.*

ASSEMBLING THE 1903 POWERED FLYER

Top left: Assembly of the 1903 powered flyer began in early October. This image shows the extent of the construction process. Wilbur is seen in the rear, either in thought or assembling something, and Orville is in the forefront with tools in hand. *Library of Congress #656*.

Top right: This detail shows a shipping crate with the address "Wilbur Wright, Elizabeth City, North Carolina" (image rotated to improve legibility). *Hidden Image #656-001*.

Left: A close-up of Orville in the foreground and Wilbur in the background, as they are assembling the 1903 flyer. Note Orville's use of sophisticated woodworking tools. *Hidden Image #656-003*.

Below: Orville with chisel and impressive hand drill. *Hidden Image #656-004*.

Opposite bottom left: The workbench with a large metal vise and various tools. *Hidden Image #656-002*.

Opposite bottom right: A ready broom and support braces for the 1902 building. *Hidden Image #656-005*.

READY FOR FLIGHT—24 NOVEMBER 1903

Left: In this image of 24 November 1903, the second round of propeller shafts has been installed and all is ready for a flight test. Wilbur poses in front of the 1903 hangar building looking at his work of engineering and art. *Library of Congress #606*.

Below: Close-up of Wilbur in preparation for flight. *Hidden Image #606-001*.

Left: A second image before the 1903 hangar, almost identical to the preceding image. Library of Congress #607.

Below: Another look at Wilbur as he prepares for flight on 24 November. Hidden Image 607-001.

READY FOR FLIGHT—14 DECEMBER 1903

Left: With a third set of propeller shafts installed, on 14 December the Wrights prepared for a test flight. They placed their launching track on the slope of Big Kill Devil Hill. Then just before starting the flight the Kill Devil Hill lifesavers arrived and helped them put the plane on the track. Two of the lifesavers brought sons and one a dog. One tantalizing facet of this photograph is that in the upper right-hand corner just over the horizon is a mystery individual barely visible. The identity of this individual is not known, nor what he was doing on Big Kill Devil Hill that day. Notice the footmarks leading to the pre-flight position. *Library of Congress #612*.

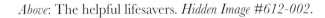

Above: The helpful lifesavers. *Hidden Image #612-002*.

Bottom far right: The boys and the dog. *Hidden Image #612-001*.

Bottom middle: The mystery man of Kill Devil Hills. *Hidden Image #612-003*.

POWERED FLIGHT, 1903

Left: In this image, almost identical to the preceding and obviously taken moments later, with barely little repositioning of the lifesavers and the dog, note the "truck" used for the flyer to slide along the track. The truck was designed to drop off when the plane went aloft, much like a disposable launching rocket for a spacecraft. The "mystery man" is still visible at the top of the horizon. *Library of Congress #613.*

Bottom left: Again the dog and an inquisitive boy with his father. *Hidden Image #613-001.*

Middle right: The truck on the flyer. *Hidden Image #613-003.*

Far right bottom: In this blurry detail, the mystery man can still be seen lurking on the horizon. *Hidden Image #613-004.*

TRACK OF FAILED FLIGHT

On 14 December, with the launching track and truck in place, the test began. This photograph shows the track and the deposited truck following the attempted flight. *Library of Congress #609*.

POWERED FLIGHT, 1903

Though the truck worked perfectly, the plane and its operators did not. *Hidden Image #609-001.*

A close-up view of the track and the truck. *Hidden Image #609-002.*

WILBUR GROUNDED

Left: The 14 December flight was not successful. After a 3.5-second flight of 105 feet the plane dived to the ground. Note the shadow of the photographer taking the picture. *Library of Congress #610.*

Below: Close-up of Wilbur at the end of the failed flight. *Hidden Image #610-001.*

POWERED FLIGHT, 1903

READINESS FOR FLIGHT—17 DECEMBER 1903

Left: On 17 December, the day of reckoning had arrived. After a few repairs, again with the assistance of lifesavers from the Kill Devil station, the powered flyer was put in place on the track. The track was moved from the slope to flat ground. *Library of Congress #615.*

Below: In this detail, the truck can be seen quite well. *Hidden Image #615-001.*

THE FIRST FLIGHT

Left: The first flight on 17 December 1903 at 10:35 a.m.—perhaps the most famous and widely copied photograph in human history. Rising from a level surface with Orville at the controls, the truck has dropped off at the end of the track, *Library of Congres #626*.

Below: A close-up of the truck. *Hidden Image #626-003*.

POWERED FLIGHT, 1903

Top left: To the right of the truck is a bench, used as a steadying device, with a handsome C-clamp used to fix one of the flyer's wings. *Hidden Image #626-004.*

Top right: The magneto was used for starting the engine. Also present are a shovel for burrowing the track and steadying devices and a bucket of grease for slathering the moving parts of the flyer's engine and drive system. *Hidden Image #626-002.*

Below: Close-up of Wilbur near the whirring propellers of the first flight. *Hidden Image #626-001.*

THE FOURTH FLIGHT

Left: This image shows the end of the fourth and most successful flight on 17 December, piloted by Wilbur for 852 feet over a period of 59 seconds. *Library of Congress #629*.

Below: Wilbur, Orville and an observer at the end of the fourth flight on 17 December 1903. *Hidden Image #629-001*.

THE DAMAGED CRAFT

Above: A photograph of the 1903 flyer after its landing from the fourth flight on 17 December. A lifesaver looks on at the damaged craft from the left corner of the picture. *Library of Congress #614.*

Right: The unidentified lifesavers look over the wreck of the fourth flight on 17 December 1903. *Hidden Image #614-001.*

BYE BYE KITTY HAWK

Left: As Wilbur and Orville left Kitty Hawk on 21 December 1903, they looked back on the realm of their recent achievements, taking this photograph from Roanoke Sound. A detail shows Kill Devil Hills in the midst of this long view. *Library of Congress #624.*

Below: Close-up of Kill Devil Hills from Manteo on 21 December 1903. *Hidden Image #624-001.*

FLIGHT ENUNCIATED WORLDWIDE
1908

The Wrights did not return to Kitty Hawk again for flights until 1908. During 1904 and 1905 they conducted tests at Huffman Prairie, eight miles outside of what was then the city limits of Dayton. Although they declared the place to be far inferior to Kitty Hawk in terms of wind, spaciousness and soft sand landings, this confined space forced them to practice takeoffs and landings and controlled flight within strict limits that they would not have had to deal with in their North Carolina laboratory.

At the end of the 1905 flying the brothers were convinced that they had a perfected flying machine and that they should stop flying and start attempting to sell their invention to the United States government and perhaps also various governments in Europe. For the next two years, Orville and Wilbur were thus busy securing patents not only in the United States but also in France, Germany, Austria, Italy and the United Kingdom, and they entered into negotiations with all of these governments. During 1907 both Wilbur and Orville began traveling across Europe trying to seal agreements.

In early 1908 everything fell into place. The Wrights secured a contract to supply the U.S. Army Signal Corps with a flyer for $25,000. They also signed a French contract to deliver a plane that could achieve certain specifications for flight: endurance, height, weight carried and other details. These performance standards had to be demonstrated in public flights in both the United States and France by September 1908.

To prepare for these tests the Wrights decided to return to Kitty Hawk in April and May 1908 and there test their revamped 1905 flyer for performance of the required standards. Wilbur went to Kitty Hawk 6 April and, of course, planned to do some new construction on their buildings. Orville did not follow until 21 April, arriving at Kitty Hawk on 25 April, the same day as the shipped flyer. A quiet week was spent assembling the plane.

Then suddenly the past peaceful solitude of Kitty Hawk was invaded. A reporter from Norfolk, Virginia, operating on rumors of the brothers' presence at Kitty Hawk, began fabricating sensational stories of their flights—even before they flew. His dispatches brought forth a deluge of reporters from New York and London.

While the Wrights only actually flew for a week—very successfully—from 6 to 14 May, the reporters arrived in time to witness several of the greatest flights and to send accurate dispatches to the world's presses. The Wrights were at first distressed, but then seemed to take it in stride as good for their cause of selling their flying machine.

Wilbur departed Kitty Hawk 17 May, on his way to New York and from there to France. Orville left four days later on his way to Washington, D.C., to inspect his proving grounds. It was thus from Kitty Hawk in 1908 that the age of flight, long rumored, was enunciated worldwide.

[Author's Note: *Unfortunately the Wrights were successful in making very few photographs in 1908. This was because, as Orville later explained to a correspondent, a hole was punctured in the bellows of their camera, which went unnoticed until they got back to Dayton. Since the Wrights took all of their negatives—film or glass plates—back with them to Dayton, they didn't know whether they had good pictures, or even any pictures, until they developed and printed them themselves back home.*]

THE 1908 HEADQUARTERS BUILDING

Left: In this image the new 1908 Wright headquarters building is on the right and the wrecked 1903 building on the left. In the new building there are windows and a sliding front door. Between the two buildings, clearly visible in the distance, is an excellent view of Kill Devil Hills Lifesaving Station and adjacent buildings. Telegraph poles connecting the station to other stations along the coast can be seen very faintly. *Library of Congress #671.*

Right: Beside the new 1908 building are two dollies, used by the Wrights to roll out their improved 1905 flyer, which was much heavier than the 1903 flyer. The brothers developed the dollies using the same design as that employed by the lifesavers for rolling out their heavy surf boats. *Hidden Image #671-002.*

Opposite page first: A view of Kill Devil Hills Station in the distance. *Hidden Image #671-003.*

Opposite page second: Kill Devil Hills landscape. *Hidden Image #671-004.*

Opposite page third: Kill Devil Hills Station on the horizon. *Hidden Image #671-005.*

Opposite page fourth: Between piles of discarded lumber and beams may be seen an excellent image of the Kill Devil Hills Lifesaving Station. *Hidden Image #671001.*

DOLLIES FOR TRANSPORTING AIRCRAFT

Left: A slightly altered perspective from the previous image. The dollies have been repositioned and their similarity to lifesaving dollies is even more apparent. *Library of Congress #672*.

Below: An exceedingly clear view of the 1908 dollies. *Hidden Image #672-001*.

Above: In this detail it is clear that the Wrights put on roofing paper as neatly as they did the knots and rivets in their flying machines *Hidden Image #672-003*.

Right: A close-up view of the front of the building reveals a barrel for collecting water, a roll of tar paper and the sliding door. *Hidden Image #672-002*.

THE STORM-DAMAGED 1903 CAMP

Left: From the other side of the camp we can see the storm-damaged remains of the 1903 building and of the 1902 glider that had been stored therein. Debris from the devastation of storms has already been neatly piled for whatever project the Wrights might next pursue. *Library of Congress #673*.

Right: Close-up of the destroyed 1903 building and the remains of the 1902 flyer. *Hidden Image #673-001*.

THE KILL DEVIL HILLS CAMP, 1908

Left: A view of the 1908 camp from Big Kill Devil Hill. This is the only distant view of the camp from 1908. The quality of the photograph suggests the impending failure of their camera. *Library of Congress #675.*

Bottom left: Close-up of the 1908 camp building. *Hidden Image #675-001.*

Bottom right: Close-up of abandoned 1903 building. *Hidden Image #675-002.*

HIDDEN IMAGES

WILBUR TRACKS AWAY BEFORE FLIGHT

Left: This is the only surviving photograph made by the Wrights of their attempted flights in 1908. Wilbur seems to be tracking away from the 1905 flyer, while three lifesavers in their summer white uniforms rest in the sand awaiting instructions or action. *Library of Congress #669.*

Bottom left: For unknown reasons, Wilbur distances himself from the flyer in May 1908. Lifesavers in their white uniforms watch the activities. *Hidden Image #669-001.*

Bottom right: Orville is at work at the center of the 1905 flyer making it ready for a first flight. *Hidden Image #669-002.*

A 1908 KILL DEVIL HILLS LANDSCAPE

This is the only view of the 1908 landscape recorded by the Wrights. Big Kill Devil Hill and its surroundings were just as rugged as ever. In this image the Wrights seem to have wanted to capture the tundra, the marsh, the scrub brush and the majestic hill. *Library of Congress #674.*

THE SOARING PLACE REVISITED
1911

From the moment Wilbur and Orville left Kitty Hawk in May 1908 they were world-renowned characters. By September of that year Wilbur was setting world records for speed, altitude and length of flight almost daily in France. And often the next day Orville would exceed Wilbur's records at Fort Myer, Virginia, before a cadre of U.S. Army officers and reporters.

For Daytonians, for Kitty Hawkers, for Americans and, indeed, for people all over the Western world, it had to be one of the most intoxicating times in history. Just a few years before there were only rumors that men could fly and there were thousands of dismal public failed attempts. Then suddenly these youthful Americans emerged as seeming experts of flight.

In both Europe and America the Wrights were glorified, cartooned and eulogized—more than anyone had been since Benjamin Franklin landed in France in early 1777 as America's foremost genius of science and invention. The Wrights used their fame to reinforce patents, contracts and new opportunities. But hardly had they won this renown when rivals emerged to challenge the patents, to claim that they could build a better plane and to resent the control the Wrights tried to exercise over all flight in Europe and America. When the Wrights tried to legally enforce their patent claims over others beginning in 1909, their jealous rivals—including the kindly Chanute, the unscrupulous Herring and the former good friend Spratt—questioned their motives and joined in criticism of the Wrights.

By 1911 Wilbur Wright was spending virtually all of his time in litigation, giving depositions, testifying in court and writing biting critiques of those people he and Orville thought were infringing their patents in Europe and America. Since the Wrights thought they should be paid royalties for every public flight of a plane in America, the number of cases to be pursued had become quite numerous.

Nevertheless, the Wrights dearly wanted to return to Kitty Hawk in 1911 and pursue something else that had obsessed them when they first arrived in North Carolina in 1900: they wanted to soar like birds. And they believed that by 1911 they had perfected flight so well that with the proper glider they could then definitely soar.

Orville designed and built the new glider for the 1911 test flights. He invited Alexander Ogilvie, a British pilot working on Wright planes in the United Kingdom, to go to Kitty Hawk for these new test flights. When it came time to head to Kitty Hawk in October 1911 for the tests, Wilbur had just filed a batch of depositions in the biggest of their lawsuits, *Wright Company v. Herring-Curtiss Company*, and the trial was getting underway. Wilbur thus remained in New York for the litigation while Orville and Ogilvie went to Kitty Hawk for the new, unprecedented tests in unpowered flight.

Orville, accompanied by brother Lorin, nephew Horace and Ogilvie, headed from Dayton to Kitty Hawk on 7 October 1911. Upon their arrival they, of course, had to build a new building and finish it up in a tidy new fashion. Beginning on 16 October and continuing until 26 October, Orville and Ogilvie pursued more than ninety glider flights.

On 18 and 23 October Orville suffered crashes, but only the craft was damaged, not him. And then on 24 October Orville established a new soaring time record of nine minutes, forty-five seconds in a fifty-mile-per-hour wind. The record stood for more than ten years.

HIDDEN IMAGES

PANORAMA OF THE 1911 CAMP

Left: This extraordinary photograph —a basic panorama of the 1911 Wright camp—is an excellent guide to the setting. The 1911 building has more windows and a better performing sliding door than its earlier counterparts. In the details of this photograph can be seen a flagpole with a windsock on top. The building is well reinforced with poles from every direction. Also in view the 1911 Wright glider. Through the wings of the glider one can see the "one-holer" privy of the 1911 camp. But the most delightful detail is of the almost obscured Orville Wright, clad in a Mexican hat, draped over the wing of the glider plugging away with a cross peen hammer used in upholstery to secure fabrics to wood subsurfaces. *Library of Congress #705.*

Bottom left: Orville hammering away attaching fabric to wood on the 1911 glider. *Hidden Image #705-001.*

Bottom right: The reinforced 1911 building with flag pole and wind sock next door. *Hidden Image #705-002.*

BUSTER WRIGHT AND THE 1911 HANGAR

Above: Horace "Buster" Wright, son of Lorin and a favorite nephew of Orville, in another view of the 1911 building. In this image he stands under the opening where the Wrights stored and brought out the 1911 glider in inclement weather. The 1911 flyer can be seen at the end of the building. Buster, of course, is wearing his own Mexican-style hat, which proved to be standard fashion in the 1911 camp. *Library of Congress #700*.

Right: Close-up of Buster Wright with his own Mexican hat. *Hidden Image #700-001*.

CAMP LIFE IN 1911

Above: Life about the 1911 camp. Buster is chasing the chickens that run free in the camp. In previous years the Wrights cooped their chickens. Also in good view is the 1911 "one-holer" privy. It is not believed that the Wrights had a privy up through 1903. Due to the lack of pictures in 1908, whether they had a previous privy is unknown. But obviously with the presence of so many reporters and observers in 1911, a privy became desirable. *Wright State #42.10*.

Right: Detail of the 1911 "one-holer." *Hidden Image #42.10 D1*.

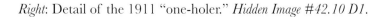

THE GUN-TOTING ORVILLE

Above: Another little-known fact about the Wrights is their views about guns. In this 1911 photograph Orville is shown in the kitchen cleaning his rifle. The Wrights always had guns with them at Kitty Hawk. On frequent occasions they competed in target practice; they shot birds for food; they tried to scare away stray pigs. At one point in 1902 Orville became so annoyed with a mouse in their building that he fired at the mouse and missed, but put a good-size hole in the side of the building. *Wright State #42.14.*

Right: Orville with his rifle in 1911. *Hidden Image #42.14 D1.*

PHOTO OPPORTUNITY №1

Left: Even before Orville and Ogilvie could get off the ground, a host of photographers and reporters descended upon the camp at Big Kill Devil Hill. In order to satisfy their wishes for a story and photographs, Orville granted two photo opportunities, recorded in this photograph and the next, taken by Lorin Wright (note his shadow). In this one Orville and Ogilvie are adjusting the controls on the glider while the photographers at both wing tips shoot pictures. The short individual in the white cap and jacket is "Uncle" Bennie O'Neal from the Kill Devil Hills Lifesaving Station. The group off to the side are evidently other onlookers. *Library of Congress #693*.

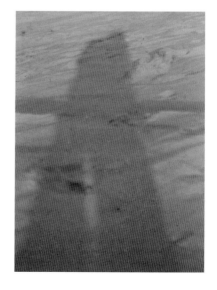

Right: Lorin Wright's shadow as photographer. *Hidden Image #693-001*.

Top left: Photographer at the 1911 photo opportunity. *Hidden Image #693-002.*

Top right: These reporters are having a private confab away from the photo situation. *Hidden Image #693-004.*

Bottom right: Another photographer taking advantage of the rare photo opportunity. *Hidden Image #693-003.*

PHOTO OPPORTUNITY №2

Left: Similar to preceding image photographers portrayed here are having a field day. But Orville has moved to the end of the glider and is holding it in place. In one detail a white sandbag can be seen in front of the plane, used for ballast. *Library of Congress #698.*

Right: Orville holds down the 1911 glider, which is about to take off on its own accord, and a reporter helps. Uncle Bennie O'Neal seems a little discombobulated with hands in his pockets. *Hidden Image #698-003.*

Left: Van Ness Harwood of the *New York World* with a bulging copy of the *Virginian Pilot* in his left coat pocket. *Hidden Image #698-001.*

Above: Bumpass of a news photographer outfitted with fancy galoshes to prevent sand penetration to the feet. The sandbag used for ballast is evident at the front of the craft. *Hidden Image #698-002.*

ORVILLE SOARS

Above: Finally, Orville soars with sandbag protruding from front of the plane and the Atlantic surf in the distance. *Library of Congress #699*.

Right: Close-up of Orville soaring with sand bag forward of the craft. *Hidden Image #699-001*.

THE SOARING PLACE REVISITED, 1911

OBSERVERS ARE MESMERIZED

Left: A reporter, a photographer and Uncle Bennie O'Neal watch Orville soar above Big Kill Devil Hill. *Library of Congress #692*.

Bottom right: Orville in his record 1911 glider flight. *Hidden Image #692-002*.

Bottom left: Two observers and Uncle Bennie O'Neal watch the 1911 record flight. *Hidden Image #692001*.

PARSON AND ELDER IN THE WHIRLWIND

Left: Orville soars over an onlooking audience amidst a wind storm on 26 October 1911. On the back of a print from this photograph, Orville identified the two dapper gentlemen holding their hats as "Pastor & Presiding Elder of the M.E. Church," the Methodist Episcopal Church in Kitty Hawk. *Library of Congress #708.*

Below: Close-up of the pastor and presiding elder, a playful child and another prone observer. *Hidden Image #708-001.*

VIEW FROM THE 1911 HANGAR

Left: This view from the 1911 building looks out through the canopy. The view is north, away from Big Kill Devil Hill. Note the storage of supplies in a box on the left above the canopy. *Library of Congress #706*.

Below: Detail of ceiling in hangar showing storage area with an indecipherable commercial box. *Hidden Image #706-001*.

POSING WITH THE PRESS

In another bow to the press, Orville, after his successful flights, poses with the principal reporters covering the 1911 glider flights. The individuals identified in this photograph are as follows: *Seated left to right*: Horace "Buster" Wright; Orville Wright; Alexander Ogilvie. *Standing left to right*: Lorin Wright; Van Ness Harwood, *New York World*; —— Berges, photographer for *New York American*; Arnold Kruckman, *New York American*; —— Mitchell, *New York Herald*; and John Mitchell, Associated Press. *Library of Congress #697.*

Close-up of the reporters, photographers and the Wrights. *Hidden Image #697-001.*

Left: Camera of Berges from *New York American*. *Hidden Image #697-003.*

Center: Photo case of Mitchell from *New York Herald*. *Hidden Image #697-002.*

Right: John Mitchell from the Associated Press. *Hidden Image #697-004.*

THE TELLTALE DOOR

Above: Poignant reminders of the Wright brothers at Kitty Hawk may be found in this final photograph of the 1911 camp. Through the tail of the glider may be seen the privy—here leaning from much use—and a shipping crate mailed to themselves. Most symbolic of all is the door of the 1911 hangar, with a board from another shipping crate. In lieu of a sign the board tells the story: "Wright Bros./Elizabeth City NC." *Library of Congress #703*.

Right: The leaning one-holer privy. *Hidden Image #703-001*.

Left: The telltale door, "Wright Bros./Elisabeth City, NC." *Hidden Image #703-003.*

Below: A shipping crate the brothers had mailed to themselves at Kitty Hawk. *Hidden Image #703-002.*

FAREWELL TO BIG KILL DEVIL HILL

Left: Before their final departure from Kitty Hawk in 1911, Orville was compelled to take one final photograph of Big Kill Devil Hill, the scene of his and Wilbur's triumphs. The Kill Devil Hills Lifesaving Station is barely visible from this shot taken far from their camp. The next time Orville would see Kill Devil Hills, they would no longer be sand; they would be planted over in preparation for the construction of a national memorial in honor of the two brothers who taught the world to fly. *Library of Congress #711*.

Right: A barely visible image of the Kill Devil Hills Lifesaving Station at the conclusion of all the Wright brothers' tests at Kitty Hawk, North Carolina, taken in 1911. *Hidden Image #711-001*.

AFTERWORD

Perhaps the most apt conclusion to the story told in this book of hidden images are three additional pictures:

WILBUR, CONTEMPLATOR

Wilbur Wright, as he was in much of his all too short, but incredibly productive life—deep in thought. *Undated photograph, Wright State University.*

ORVILLE, REFLECTOR

Orville Wright, seen here in his later life, sitting in his boat at his Lambert Island retreat on Georgian Bay in Canada. The name of the boat was *Kitty Hawk*. *Undated photograph, Wright State University.*

Afterword

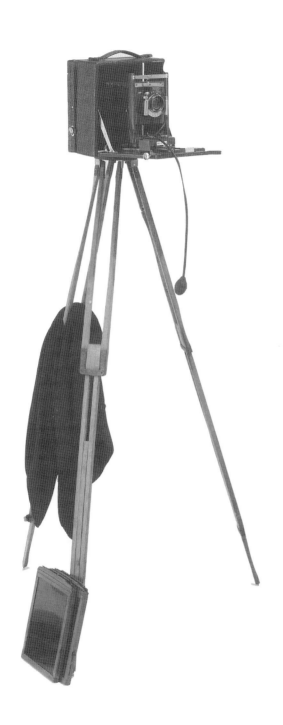

The Wright Camera. What was the most important piece of equipment the Wright brothers took with them to Kitty Hawk? *Undated photograph, Wright State University.*

INDEX

ABOUT THE AUTHOR

Dr. Larry E. Tise is an author and historian living and working in Philadelphia. Due to his unique research of the lives of the Wright brothers, he was appointed Wilbur and Orville Wright Visiting Distinguished Professor at East Carolina University for the years 2000 to the present. From 1999 until 2003 he also served as consulting historian for the North Carolina First Flight Centennial Commission, the official body that planned the 2003 commemoration of the Wright brothers' historic first powered flight on 17 December 1903. Concurrently, Tise completed three summer faculty fellowships at NASA Langley Research Center, which he has also advised on matters relating to the Wright brothers and the origins of manned flight.

Born in Winston-Salem, North Carolina, and with degrees from Duke University (AB, 1965; MDiv, 1968) and the University of North Carolina at Chapel Hill (PhD, 1974), Tise has spent much of his career as a history executive, serving as executive director of the North Carolina Division of Archives and History (1975–81), of the Pennsylvania Historical and Museum Commission (1981–87), the American Association for State and Local History in Nashville, Tennessee (1987–89), and the Benjamin Franklin National Memorial in Philadelphia, Pennsylvania (1989–96).

He was the founder and first president of the International Congress of Distinguished Awards (incorporated in 1994), a capacity he still holds. This is a consortium of organizations that present some of the world's most important awards. Tise also advises foundations, corporations and individuals in the establishment of distinguished awards for human achievement in the arts, humanities, sciences, technology, education, peace and other humanitarian endeavors.

He is completing several years of research on two major works about Wilbur and Orville Wright—both of which contain hundreds of documents written by the brothers, their family, friends, colleagues and rivals, which had never before been published. The first of these contains hundreds of documents not previously in publication written by the brothers from Kitty Hawk, their official visitors to Kitty Hawk, by Kitty Hawker residents and dozens of others—family and would-be aviators—desperately wanting to know about their successes on the North Carolina Outer Banks. The second of these projects is a collection of the family correspondence between and among the brothers, their stern and somewhat humorless father and their vibrant sister Katharine. Taken together these two publications contain hundreds of letters and photographs of social, cultural and intellectual importance that were set aside when an edition of *The Papers of Wilbur and Orville Wright* was issued by the Library of Congress on the fiftieth anniversary of the first flight in 1953.

Tise is the author of more than fifty articles and books on many facets of history and historical work, including *Proslavery: A History of the Defense of Slavery, 1700–1840* (1987), *The American Counterrevolution: A Retreat from Liberty, 1783–1800* (1999), and *Benjamin Franklin and Women* (2000). He is currently writing a sequel to *American Counterrevolution* covering the period 1800–1848 and a reference book on the world's most distinguished awards. In his work as an independent historian he conducts historical research and provides history services for clients in the United States, Canada, Europe and the West Indies.